ROUND EYES

An Adopted Child's View of Love

Written by Ginger Sanders
Illustrated by Tracy Applewhite Broome

Copyright © 2013

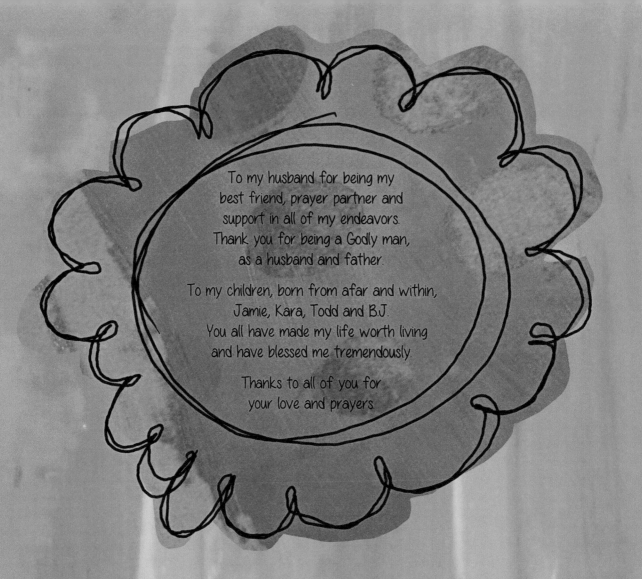

To my husband for being my
best friend, prayer partner and
support in all of my endeavors.
Thank you for being a Godly man,
as a husband and father.

To my children, born from afar and within,
Jamie, Kara, Todd and B.J.
You all have made my life worth living
and have blessed me tremendously.

Thanks to all of you for
your love and prayers.

CROSSBOOKS

CrossBooks™
A Division of LifeWay
1663 Liberty Drive
Bloomington, IN 47403
www.crossbooks.com
Phone: 1-866-879-0502

Unless otherwise noted, Scripture quotations
are from the Holy Bible, New International
Version, Copyright © 1973, 1978, 1984
by International Bible Study.

Because of the dynamic nature of the Internet, any web
addresses or links contained in this book may have changed
since publication and may no longer be valid. The views
expressed in this work are solely those of the author and
do not necessarily reflect the views of the publisher, and
the publisher hereby disclaims any responsibility for them.

ISBN: 978-1-4627-2852-7 (sc)
ISBN: 978-1-4627-2853-4 (e)

First published by CrossBooks 7/23/2013

Printed in the United States of America.

This book is printed on acid-free paper.

Art and Graphics by Tracy Applewhite Broome
tracybroome.com

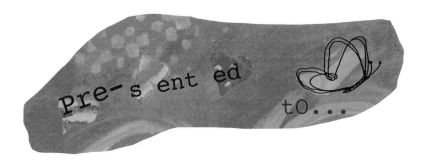

Pre-s ent ed

to....

By>

There once was a Mommy and Daddy that lived in a house,
with a big yard and a big dog named Lady,
but one thing was missing.

There were no little
boys or girls living there
in the house with the Mommy
and Daddy. The Mommy and
Daddy wanted a little boy or girl,
but did not have one.

The dog, Lady, had puppies and Lady seemed content and happy, but Mommy and Daddy did not have children.

They were lonely and wanted to share
the love and the life God had given them.

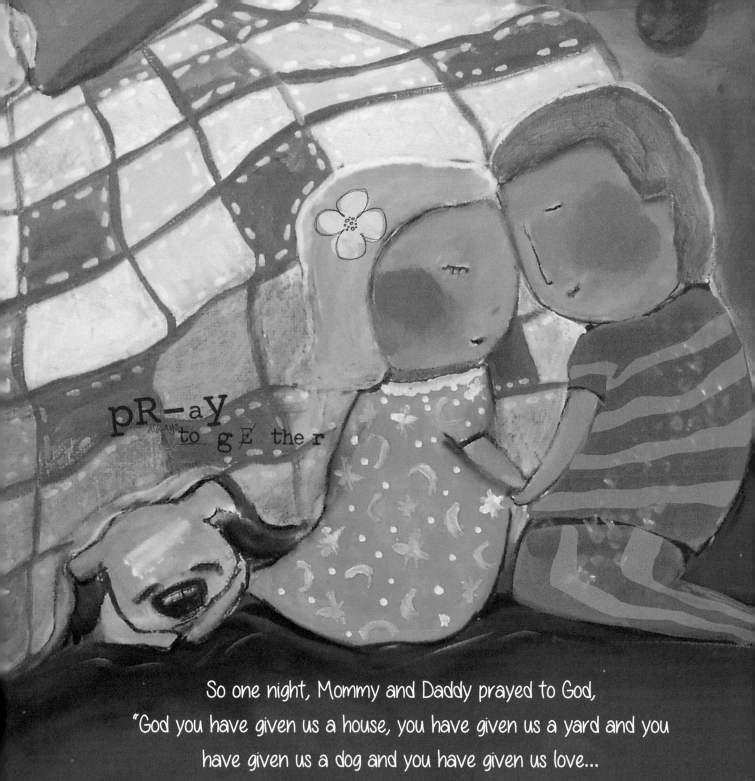

pR-aY always to gE ther

So one night, Mommy and Daddy prayed to God,
"God you have given us a house, you have given us a yard and you
have given us a dog and you have given us love...

but you haven't given
us a little boy or girl to share
any of those things with. Could
you please hear our prayers
and bless us with a child?"

In another land, far away, a little boy was born to a mother who did not have a house, or a yard, or a dog, but even though she loved her son, she could not keep him.

Jer-E mIah 29:11

precious
baby

She needed to find him a home. She prayed to God,
"God, can you find someone to love and raise my son?"

Through those prayers, though miles and miles away, God put the little boy on an airplane and he flew halfway around the world to his new Mommy and Daddy, house, yard, dog and her puppies.

They were all so very happy!

Then, one day the little boy drew a picture of his family...
stick Mommy and Daddy with great big round eyes and he was the baby
with little slanted eyes.

They all laughed, because even though they looked different,
they all shared the house, the yard, the dogs and most of all...
Love.

God's love

I John 4:7-8
Beloved, let us love one another,
for love is from God, and whoever loves has been born
of God and knows God. Anyone who does not love does
not know God, because God is love.

Can you draw your family here?

Our Story

_____

_____

_____

_____

_____

_____

_____

_____

_____

_____

_____

Round Eyes is a beautifully written story to help young readers understand the love of family—even when you do not look the same. Ginger Sanders has captured with great tenderness how it is a love and shared experiences that connect a family—in spite of differences. This sweet little book will be loved by children and their parents—for the life lesson it holds, whether or not they are adopted!

Susan Soonkeum Cox *is Vice President of Holt International Children's Services. She is recognized as a national expert on intercountry adoption and was one of the first children adopted from Korea in 1956.*

CPSIA information can be obtained
at www.ICGtesting.com
Printed in the USA
LVIC07n1636170813
348143LV00003BB